Return to Innocence

Reminders from Spirit

Cheryl Lunar Wind & Friends

Return to Innocence

Reminders from Spirit

Copyright © 2024 by Cheryl Lunar Wind

Cheryl's poetry in this collection may be shared, printed with credit given to the author. All other contributors keep rights to their work.

Any Inquiries contact:

cheryl.hiller@yahoo.com

Some of the poems in this collection first appeared in Know Your Way, Love Unconditional and We Are One chapbooks; Mount Shasta Bioregional Ecology Center newsletter; and on facebook.

Front cover photo Mother Earth, online.

First edition.

Published by Alexander Agency Books, Mount Shasta, California 96067

ISBN 979-8-9897287-3-2

Return to Innocence

Reminders from Spirit

Flowers every night
Blossom in the sky
Peace in the Infinite,
At peace am I.
   --Rumi

Preface

A few words on the practice of peace-- in the 11:11 Symbols book we receive this message from Holy Dove:

> *Three times a day, take ten minutes to think peaceful thoughts, to feel peaceful feelings and to act in Peace.*

Holy Dove carries to us the Peace Covenant of the Rainbow.

"You see, O Peoples, there is a Great Oceantide of Spirit washing over Mother Earth now. And as this Great Ocean of Energy, this Great White River of Spirit is a Flood of this Age, remember the Rainbow Covenant of your Peoples. Within the mouth of Grandmother Dove is that olive branch of the Rainbow of Purity, Innocence and Renewal."*

True Alchemy occurs through the practice of this Discipline of Peace.

"A New Era has dawned. The Spirit of Peace is here. Therefore, O Peoples, call upon the Dove Medicine, call upon Grandmother Dove, and she will come to you, circling you in the descending Spirals of Life. Then you will arise in the Ascending Spiral within your own lifestream, bringing unto your heart, bringing unto your mind, the Sacred Power which you seek."*

* The Symbols, The Universal Symbols and Laws of Creation:
A Divine Plan by Which One Can Live

In review;
Doves represent peace and love and the Holy Dove is a physical representation of holy spirit and the Divine.

The message she brings to us is exciting, Earth is now being flooded with photonic energies, the "Great White River of Spirit" from the universe.

We can return to the sacred and holy ways simply by sitting in peace daily. Also, by calling on the Holy Dove to assist us, we will be blessed with higher frequencies which facilitate our return to purity, innocence and renewal.

Contents

Return to Beauty 1
by Cheryl

America, it's time to Wake Up! 2, 3
by Gloria Cooper

Come On Now 4
by Susan Grace

It is what it is 5
by Cheryl

Keep the Peace 6
by Cody Ray Richardson

Change 7
by Cody Ray Richardson

When Women Were Birds 8
by Terry Tempest Williams

Red Rose Dragon by Cheryl 9

Ancient by Jennifer H. 10, 11

Giveaway by Cheryl 12, 13

Planting by Darrel Johannes 14

Big LoVe by Darrel Johannes 15

Be Real by Topher Kerby 16

Not Okay 16
by Jarod K. Anderson

Along the Way 17
by Susan Grace

A Practice of Patience 18
by Mercy Talley

4/8/2024 19
by A'Marie B. Thomas-Brown

eclipse by unknown 19

Mirror 20
by Cody Ray Richardson

Reflections by Jennifer H. 21

Innocence, Song by Cheryl 22

Childhood Smoke by Cheryl 23, 24

Wayshower by Cheryl 25

If I were a tree by Marie 26

The Fall 27
by Cody Ray Richardson

Alter Ego by Marie 28

Don't Listen 29
by Le'Vell Zimmerman

Poem for my brother 30
by Mercy Talley

Alchemy, Shining 31
by Mercy Talley

Words on Attention 32
by Le'Vell Zimmerman

Alignment by Susan Grace 33

There is only One 34
by Le'Vell Zimmerman

Wisdom of Innocence 34
by Le'Vell Zimmerman

Return to Innocence 35
by Le'Vell Zimmerman

Update by Jason Estes 36

Breath, Grace & Joy 37
by A'Marie B. Thomas-Brown

In Loving My Hurt 38
by Benjamin Prasad

Be Like Children 39
by Le'Vell Zimmerman

Las Plantas De Vida 40, 41, 42
by Cyrena Giordano/CYRENITY

Contributors page

Author page & Testimonials

Return to Beauty
by Cheryl

What does beauty mean to you?
Is beauty, as they say 'In the eye of the beholder'?
Can we truly judge what is beautiful?

The other day,
a male turkey crossed the road in front of me,
he strutted and sang the whole time.
In effect saying---
Be like me! Strut your stuff! Fan your tail!
Walk like an Egyptian!
Joseph wore a coat of many colors.
We all wear many coats.
He was hated by his brothers
because they deemed him the favorite.

There are no favorites!

We all are---
Shining, Exploding, Becoming,
Returning---

We will not need clothes, cars or passports!
Open UP---
It is time!

Grandmother Tree
Stands
Straight and Tall,
an example
for all of us.

We all are----Beauty.
Shining, Exploding, Becoming,
Returning.

America, it's time to Wake Up!
by Gloria Cooper

America. It's time. Wake Up.
We've fallen asleep to the greed, the pain, the suffering.
Public servants (sometimes act like privileged masters)
Politicize the dispersal of the People's federal and state funds.

> The constitutional Protection for Tax dollars
> was amended in 1886.

Corporations declared- *corporate personhood*.
Privatizing public land and the natural environment
has proven to be an economic-political-social nightmare.
Slipping into a corporate controlled coma, our nation
has descended into **hell's** shadowy realm of **fear**.

America rebelled against England's
Tyranny and oppression, in 1776.
Conquering their fears,

the colonists declared
social equanimity for their "kind".
In the new world, Public servants would be governed
by the People's collective will.

Unfortunately, lost in the shadows of prejudices and hate,
the People's will was (and continues to be) compromised.
Overshadowed by unhealthy competition and unresolved
social issues, the subjective authoritarian ego resurfaced.
America's self-governance is an unfulfilled dream.

America's dream of freedom
is possible with unadulterated truth,
information, and knowledge.
Education is essential, especially for the youth
disadvantaged by economic injustice.
Seizing public funds for corporate profit
or for the military/industrial complex are
contrary to that dream.

      Education empowers us to live and learn.
      Education prepares us for living a quality life.
      Education separates political fiction from universal truths.

America. It's time. Wake Up!
(The revolution has started.)
We are humanity, born sovereign and free.
We are sentient life expressing the heavenly art
of being. We Americans come together to ascend
with joy and creative expression into **heaven's**
realm of unconditional **love.**

Come On Now
by Susan Grace

Heal your wounds about being the odd one out.

Let go of how you've been hurt.

Nevermind that they did it on purpose.

Your aloneness is healable.

We have new worlds to build.

You can flail and be demonstrative all you want.
And then,

Come on now.

**I am a soul of love
A heart of peace
A mind of stillness
A being of light.
--unknown**

It is what it is
by Cheryl

The foundation of peace is
Acceptance.

Beyond all doors--
there is Expansiveness.

Beyond the division of
borders, gates and locked fences--

there exists the
Innocence of
openness, feeling, kindness

Beyond the
rules, restrictions and requirements
there is
freedom, imagination and spark

Beyond all the opinions and preferences--
there is peace.

There are people that don't like me--
and that is ok.

Accepting All.
It is what it is.
Peace.

Keep the Peace
by Cody Ray Richardson

Does it disturb peace or lead to it?
Am I hiding behind peace
Is peace keeping me the same
I really don't care
I mean I have to have peace
Sometimes I disturb people's peace
It's not intentional
Sometimes mine gets disturbed
Some were intentional
Some were not
My peace was disturbed
Peace is fragile
Peace is strong
Depending on how full the peace cup is
Self care
Boundaries
Strange to disturb someones peace unintentionally
It's hard not to take things personally
Sometimes the peace integrity is low in an individual
Maybe yours is
Keep your own peace
Others feel the influence
Peace is a presence
Presence is peace
Peace needs little words
Peace takes its naps
Peace will nap with you
If it won't take a nap you can tell for sure that it's not peace
Keep the peace
Peace in ourselves
Peace in our relationships
Sometimes peace is a momentary vacation from engagement
Other times peace is forever
Choose your peace
The degree of it towards others
The degree they can offer it to you
And when there is no other option
RUN

Change
by Cody Ray Richardson

The mysterious path of healing
No straight line to something constant
Progression that has no boundaries
To be stagnant is impossible
New hurt may heal old hurt
Know that you do not know
See that you do not see
Not from the grand perspective
The perspective that matters
Lesser loves will come and go
The greater love remains
The grandiose of all relationships
The one between you and change

"The 'magic' will take over when you release the Egos expectations.
Following your excitement is to embody the **innocence** of the Higher Self.
It requires great wisdom and spiritual maturity to trust yourself at this level."
--Le'Vell Zimmerman

When Women Were Birds
by Terry Tempest Williams

Once upon a time,
when women were birds,
there was a simple understanding that
to sing at dawn and sing at dusk
was to heal the world through joy.

The birds still remember
what we have forgotten,
that the world is meant
to be celebrated.

Red Rose Dragon
by Cheryl

Water dragons live in the sea--
Air dragons hide in the clouds--
Land dragons are in nature--
places like gardens, forests and mountains.

They love the flowers, playing hide and seek with them.

Some male, some female--
they visit Earth like a field trip. (trip to the park)

I have a special dragon friend, her name is Red Rose.
She shape shifts from dragon to rose and back again.

Don't go looking for a dragon, for
they won't be found.

Wait,
and they will come to you.

Ancient by Jennifer H.

Singing to the tree--
the words, ancient and deep
from another time,
nearly forgotten, hidden, asleep.

Suddenly,
everything shifts, merges and converges.

Now,
I'm sitting in the tree,
feeling it become me.
When I open my eyes,
I'm touching the sky
The wind blowing through me as leaves on the tree
totally and utterly free.

I flow to the ground
traveling through roots
reaching out,
as far as the eye can see--
energy all connected, intertwined and integrated.

The black hills grass giggled and tickled above
as I flow through roots below.

I feel the wind again,
russling and tussling
as the Buffalo I saw a mile back
now,
stands over and on me.
Grass is a hive mind,
each blade blows singularily and together.
They giggle harmoniously.
The wind tickled
as we giggled and waved
loving to be swayed.

For a brief moment,
I feel myself rise
and see through Buffalo eyes.

Then snap,
I'm back at the tree
feeling my body, all around me
my feet planted in dirt.
Standing in sunshine,
bees singing to me.

Now,
time to move along.
Nothing can go wrong.
Time to help people live,
pure, connected and free.

Giveaway
by Cheryl

If you seek
eternal waters within--
to find---make
an offering.

Reciprocate.

Be in gratitude for all you receive.

Mother Gaia
gives
air, water and light
thru her aura.

When taking a life for nourishment---
Give thanks.
Whether it be
plant or animal.

When cutting a tree, bush or flower---
ask permission.

When life is lost because of fire---
Offer condolences.

Say a prayer--
for those killed
on the road.

When planting a garden---
ask a blessing by the insects and fairies.
They are the same.

Show honor to all life---
physical, elemental and spirit.

Mitake' Oyasin means
'All my relations.'

Life is not a pyramid--

We are not on top--

Life is a circle--
wheel--
the eternal hoop.

Wheel of Karma.

Be careful---
If you mistreat another--
you might just seal
your next life plan.

Want to know
what its like
in anothers shoes?

Ask to be shown---
thru a vision or dream.

See from their eyes.
Gain understanding.
Walk softly.
She has a way about her.
Practice the Way of Wisdom.
Be gentle with others.
Reciprocate.
Giveaway.

It is the practice of giveaway that assists the human movement into their pure heart space of innocence.

Planting
by Darrel Johannes

We plant the seeds--
of all the best times;
the creative
the most dear
honest
loving & considerate.

Those seeds that have always been
and will always be--
Are here now,
in this garden.

Our garden feels like the last chance
of goodness here on Earth.
It is here, the seeds will find ready and
fertile ground--
being watered by our grief, despair and
hopes.

The fruit of this garden will bring a
Demarcation.
Eternal order qualities
will grow.

Big LoVe
by Darrel Johannes

The ancestors all say, please
MAKE ROOM FOR ME
you need only what we have for you.

For those who have been choosing their personal comfort--
over truth and greater good,
that will no longer be supported,
in any way.

Love is Big so it has to do what it has to do.
Your smallness will no longer be an obstacle.
You can give it up in an orderly fashion, or
it will be torn from you--

We wish you no harm, but
Love of the greater good requires this.

signed--
The Elements, the Angels, the Love, Life and Spirits.

Be Real
by Topher Kerby

never be ashamed to say,
"i'm worn out. i've had
enough. i need some time
for myself."

that isn't being selfish.
that isn't being weak.

that's being human.

Not Okay
by Jarod K. Anderson

I am not okay today.
So, in the absence of okay,
what else can I be?

I can be gentle.
I can be unashamed.
I can turn my pain into connection.
I can be a student of stillness.
I can be awake to nature.
I can sharpen my empathy
against the stone of discomfort.

I am not okay,
but I am many worthy things.

Along the Way
by Susan Grace

Letting go of disappointment, shame, regret
is an active choice you can make in real time.

You don't have to dig up every single turn you've made
Along the way to get here.

You can accept that life happens how it needs to and
You've not yet seen how it all plays out.

You can be at peace with
Not knowing how it all plays out.

You can be at peace with
Not knowing how it all
eventually is adding up.

All is forgiven.
When you know better, you do better.
You are stronger every day.

All is well, no matter the actual challenge
in front of you.
Because in your lived-experience wisdom,
You trust your own empowerment.

A Process of Patience
by Mercy Talley

Retrieving
what was
held captive
in shock
embedded
trauma
triggers
a past
reoccurring
though no
longer existing
in this present
moment...
liberation
is an ongoing
process of patience
worth reacquainting
myself with All That I Am ~

4/8/2024
by A'Marie B. Thomas-Brown

Being on all fours
Eyes closed
Being rocked
From the inside out

Being in bed
Curled in a fetal position
Cradling the night
Blinded by light

Movement
Utterance
Stillness
And then there was Breath

A time Of darkness
Spiritual renewing
An opportunity for introspection
A shedding of old energies

Manifest in the eclipsing
Of our Remembrance
Of Rest
Of Peace

And, so we breathe

eclipse by unknown

Sometimes, I think of the sun and the moon as lovers who rarely meet, always chase, and almost always miss one another. But once in a while, they do catch up, and they kiss, and the world stares in awe of their eclipse.

Mirror
by Cody Ray Richardson

To fit is one way
To show us ourselves another
Easy to mimic
Brave to reflect
Each hold a different effect
Oh the perfect puzzle piece
It feels so wonderful and amazing
Is it real
Chameleons everywhere
Learned to show you what you want to see
Ask yourself is this me
Why do we fit
A reflection can be less complimenting
Still more real
More useful
Less manipulative
Some run from their reflection
Right into the fire of deception
It's only warm and comfortable in the beginning
Then the peace is bonded
Hard to escape
A mirror may bring awareness of adjustment needed
To be shown yourself is not easy
It's not easy to do either
To be brutally honest is to risk those you care about to flee
A balance of both may or may not be a option
Better to show than be a show
Better to know than live illusive
My mirror
My friend
Your as real as I am
Your honesty is a gift
A medicine not always easy to swallow
I appreciate when real meets real
To see is to know
To show at all odds is love
Once the seeing is accepted
True change begins
Much easier with another
I seek my mirror
We will stand together as long as we can stand

Reflections
by Jennifer H.

As we wonder through this world,
Life lessons flow to us
through reflections.

Most only see an ugly seer--

~things that make us want to sneer
~things that we want to fear
~things that we can't stand to feel
~things that are there for us to heal

then moving on, rather quickly
don't want to stay and
keep looking sickly

not open to the other side
of the beauty that's inside
the strength and courage
that is there is
covered over by that fear

If we'd only stop and breathe
take it all in
and let ourselves see
the Beauty in me
is in you too

Innocence
by Cheryl

You are beautiful
   like a flower.

Fragile and strong
   at the same time.

Until someone,
  comes along
  and greedily
  picks you,

leaving you to wither and die.

Song
by Cheryl

A beautiful song is
  gone too
      quickly
like youth,
and opportunity.

After while, all
  that's left
     are
memories and regret.

Childhood Smoke
by Cheryl

Are we like the flowers---
beautiful,
fragile yet strong
at the same time?
As we get older,
does the world get colder?
Like a song,
that passes too quickly?

When your mother tells you that your dad doesn't love you---
When your step-dad kicks your cat and tells you how good you look----
When you can't breathe
because of all the cigarette butts laying around---
Its
Childhood Smoke.

I remember chasing wild kittens in my Grandma's barn.
I found a 4-leaf clover that day,
and I knew all would be well.

Please, Please Momma,
don't drive so fast.

I gave my mom a hard time,
Coming,
After 3 days of labor---
Out I came, feet first---
It was like,
I knew what I was in for,
And, I had changed my mind.

The story is that my mom
threw me, as a newborn,
Perhaps I just slipped off the couch---
But my grandmother took care of me.
She was an angel,
Who now, still helps me
from her place, on the other side.

One day, my mom packed up my stuff
and dropped me off
at my dad's house---
soon after,
I woke up with his hands around my throat---

I don't know what's worse---
Not being loved by my dad---
Or being loved too much by my stepdad.

I grew up watching Gilligen's Island---
If those seven strangers could get along
on a deserted island,
then why couldn't we?

Round and Round, we go.
For a three hour tour, we go.

Where is the love and light?
We are.
We create,
by living our lives.
In fact, that is why we are here.
We are one,
of the many threads,
in this tapestry of life.

Look back to that 4-leaf clover,
We are never alone, and
We are loved.

The angels are singing---
Look at that Cheryl---
She took Childhood Smoke,
and turned it into Light.

Wayshower
by Cheryl

Sounds like a sea fairing term--
a ship, captain or traveler
by sea.

I lead the way.
I show by example.

I am just a fellow traveler
along the way
on the path
going home.

If I were a tree
by Marie

I like the way trees stand there
Blowing in the wind
Trees, are calm, cool and collected
I wish I were a tree
Standing there strong
Not having a worry
Or care in the world
I wish I were able to be that centered
Being able to change when I can
Having a fresh new start when my leaves fall for the winter
Being able to give the world air
If I were a tree
I would be one of the strongest plants
That would help people of course
A strong calm helpful tree
That's what I would be
If I were a tree

The Fall
by Cody Ray Richardson

It fell over in and around me
As loud as a Bell
As quiet as a thought
Just as pronounced
It held me in its arms
All grew around it
Everything somehow a slow release of its original gift
I wish In its falling
I suspend my troubles
In this moment I absorb its healing and loving presence
Open to knowing its consistent nature
Predictable yet I will miss it when it's away
Oh how lucky to have had another day
The illusion of going down
What does this mean for us
It is certainly extraordinary indeed
All for the growth of this planet and its guests
The simple to complicated dynamics in balance
Oh beautiful life
What are you
What is this
This presentation
This living learning show
Oh how interesting you are
Never a bore
Who cares what it's all for
Here I am
Happy to be
Of course it would be better with you
I respect the space in between the notes
The rest is my favorite
Nothing without the subtle
No definition without
The dark warm ooze of creative waters
The depths we can go
Oh what a gift
To experience this place through my body from my soul

Alter ego
by Marie

You know that inescapable feeling of anger
When you're being yelled at in particular
All you want to do is yell back
The only thing you want to do is attack
Holding it back is kind of hard
It's like trying to bury someone alive in a graveyard
Then eventually there is a spark
One that fights back like a shark
All that anger is suddenly released
Then later you may feel at ease
Or you will feel bad and regret what you said
Until you'll want to cry in your bed
not me, but I should feel like that
My reality cowards away and scurries like a rat
My alter ego is only about violence
I can't keep her contained,
I don't know why she is like this
Always there babbling in my brain
She drives me insane
But, I wonder
Does anyone else have that blunder
Or am I the only one
With a pain, that has only just begun

Don't Listen
by Le'Vell Zimmerman

It's the capacity of fear that you are entertaining within which is the foundation of all harmful experiences unfolding in your holographic experience.

Here is where you recognize the importance of cultivating a healing lifestyle through practicing more presence and stillness beyond the talking in your head.

Once again,
the true self is not the "voice in your head".

Don't Listen

-333

Poem for my Brother
by Mercy Talley

Poem for my brother
When the bruises
go unseen
kept in the corner
of a quiet
weeping heart
does it mean
they don't exist
keep up keep up
hold your head up high
pretend pretend
cover up & carry on
If it isn't seen
does it mean
it doesn't exist . .
where does he go
who does he tell
the shame it would
bring her
the relatives
could shun her
hide what mother
does when no one sees
blows to the head
send wounds to the heart
If it isn't seen
does it mean
it doesn't exist . .

Alchemy
by Mercy Talley

My voice creates an echo
through the realm of my Soul
reverberating Love's rescue
from a mind made to toil

weary tho I am
this promise soothes my Heart
Knowledge of the alchemy;

constriction to expression
density to prosperity
sorrow becoming Joy ~

Shining
by Mercy Talley

Shining With Each Other
replaces the need to
outshine
which stems from
the wounding of
not being enough ~

We Are All Enough
& Contribute So Much
by Living from Our Hearts ~

Words on Attention
by Le'Vell Zimmerman

It's called "pay attention" because it's actually an investment of your manifestation energy.

Your gift of free will allows you to decide as a Creator Being what to give energy to beloved.

Choose wisely.

The more you invest, the more likely it will manifest in your reality.

Love or Fear.

The choice is yours.

-333

The attempt to gain outer attention, approval and/or validation stems from a lack of self love and acceptance, where external reinforcement becomes an addiction which is unsustainable.

It's your responsibility to acknowledge the priceless nature of your own perfection and beauty as a manifestation of God.

Attempting to solicit the approval of others is reflective of this dependency, where such behavior is truly "unattractive".

Once again, Self Love is the foundation of all Love.

-333

Alignment
by Susan Grace

There's no drama in alignment.

It's for you - engage.
It's not for you - leave it alone.

How do you decipher between the two?

If it increases your quality of life;
If it's oddly specific to what's important to you;
If it means you're making the world a better place-

Then it's for you.

If you have to force it;
If you have to weave a story to make sense of it;
If you suspect you'll regret spending your precious time on it-

Then it's not for you.

What does your higher knowing say?

There is only One
by Le'Vell Zimmerman

The Creator doesn't "compete".

There is simply the focus on more creation.

The Sun has no competition.

There is only The One.

All else is an illusion.

Masters know.

Wisdom of Innocence
by Le'Vell Zimmerman

Your emotional/spiritual maturity is reflective in your level of patience, acceptance, and compassion for others.

Immature souls exhibit much impatience, sarcasm, and judgment as if they don't make mistakes everyday like everyone else.

All are here on the path of self realization paved in ignorance.

When your gentle with life, life will be gentle with you.

Accepting your ignorance is to align with the wisdom of innocence.

Return to Innocence
by Le'Vell Zimmerman

Aggression, impatience and other extreme emotional distortions are simply indicators of internal fear.

Not strength.

When you trust yourself, there is a calm sense of presence, empathy and compassion for yourself and all reflections as an expression of God.

Mature Leaders have the capacity to understand reflections and demonstrate the patience in which to harmoniously work with others in the refinement of a relationship, community and/or Kingdom.

It always goes back to your own capacity of trust in yourself.

This is your capacity of trust in God.

-333

Trust, self love and compassion create the field of understanding that allows us to move from fear to love. In that state of vulnerability we can Return to Innocence.

Update
by Jason Estes

As we progress into April,

Remember that judgment is a weapon that only ever hurts you and acceptance is the key that sets you free to make new choices ... often our triggered state makes up judgments to slow us down so we can find ourselves again, but our acceptance unlocks infinite potential ...

Remember, acceptance is not the same thing as agreeing ...
as you travel through the rest of 2024, one of the biggest keys is acceptance ...
without it, most of the year will feel like it is evil, bad, or wrong, or happening to you not for you ...

Remember, this is a clean-up year, so accept what is, where it is, and then allow it to change in front of your eyes ...

When we truly enter a state of acceptance, the world naturally unlocks and changes and heals, and there is very little effort required ...

Remember,
we are more powerful then we can imagine and we are teaming up now ... so the world will drastically change in the direction we choose as a team ... so let's remove division and judgment and work on ourselves ... let that echo out into the world and be the change we want to see ...

Breath, Grace & Joy
By A'Marie B. Thomas-Brown

Show up for you.

We fear what we do not understand,
forgetting that what goes up, must come down;
what swings left, will swing right.

Time heals and reveals.

We all have the same ending and beginning,
it is our unique experience that colors
the field and gives rise to That Which Is.

We are equipped. We are able. We can. And we will.

Wholeness calls to us because we are already whole.

Be grateful that you are here with such multiplicities and opportunities. Be your self and know thy Self. Two sides of the same coin. Good and evil, death and life meld into Light.

We have Breath. We have Grace. We have Joy.

May every experience bring us to deeper depths and higher breadths as we navigate and propagate change within and in relation with All That Is.

Be amazed. Follow peace. Lead with love.

In Loving My Hurt
by Benjamin Prasad

I fought my pain and lost.

I judged my pain,
and believed it was hurting me.

When I learned
That my pain
Was not my suffering

That my suffering
Was my resistance to my pain

I ran alongside my resistance.
I befriended the part of me that said, again and again,
"I f-ing hate this."

I chose to agree
with the authentic truth
In what I really hated about my pain.

And my resistance agreed
And it felt good to cry again.

To be only with the initial hurt
Feels like love.

To be in resistance
to the resistance to the anger about the hurt
Feels like brutal suffering

I'm softer now.

I can welcome in more of what's sad
Because I'm suffering it less.

Be Like Children
by Le'Vell Zimmerman

Over analysis has a way of causing deep anxiety amongst what is a blessing to you.

For example; a joyful swim in the pool is "ruined" by fear when the logical Ego mind is worried about "what's in it" on a microscopic level.

Once again, you get to decide to enjoy the blessing of being alive or not beloved.

Your spiritual maturity is reflective in what you choose to give energy to.

Truly awakened souls know they are safe "to play" amongst their own innocence within this holographic experience.

Masters know this.

-3333

Truly Wonderful, the mind of a child is.

Fear is ignorant.

Love is intelligent.

This holographic experience is much more complex than the logical mind can comprehend.

Your innocence is extremely powerful, where you have access to that which the logical mind may assume is "impossible".

Healing is a choice beloved.

-3333

Las Plantas De Vida
by Cyrena Giordano/CYRENITY

Las Plantas de Vida de este Medicina se cantan
Ooo se cantan
Las Plantas de Vida de este Medicina se cantan
Ooo se cantan,
Ooo se cantan,
Ooo se cantan,
Ooo se cantan,

Dicen que todo es curando, que todo es curando

Dicen que todo es amor,
que todo es amor, que todo es amor

Dicen que si puedes sentirte,
si puedes sentirte , si puedes sentir

Dicen que todo en balancia,
que todo en balancia,
que todo en balancia,
que todo en balancia,
que todo en balancia

Dicen que todo de provecho,
que todo de provecho,
que todo de provecho,
que todo de provecho,
que todo de provecho,
que todo de provecho.

The plants of this Life of this Medicine
they sing to me, ooo they sing to me.
The plants of this Life of this Medicine they tell me,
Ooo they tell me, Ooo they tell me,
Ooo they sing to me, Ooo they sing to me.

They say that everything is healing,
that everything is healing.

They say that all of it is love,
that all of it is love, that all of it is love.

They say don't be afraid of feeling,
don't be afraid of feeling,
that it's okay to feel.

They say that it's all in the balance,
it's all in the balance, it's all in the balance.

They say that everything is worthy,
that everything is worthy,
that everything is worthy,
that everything is worthy,
that everything is worthy.

La Planta de Vida de este Medicina se canta
Ooo se canta
La Planta de Vida de este Medicina se canta
Ooo se canta,
Ooo se canta,
Ooo se canta,
Ooo se canta,

Dice que todo es curando,
Que todo es curando
Dice que todo es amor,
Que todo es amor, que todo es amor

Dice que si puedes sentirte,
si puedes sentirte , si puedes sentir

Dice que todo en balancia,
que todo en balancia,
que todo en balancia,
que todo en balancia,
que todo en balancia.

Dice que todo de provecho,
que todo de provecho,
que todo de provecho,
que todo de provecho,
que todo de provecho,
que todo de provecho.

The Plant of this Life of this Medicine she sings to me,
ooo she sings to me.
The Plant of this Life of this Medicine she tells me,
ooo she tells me, ooo she tells me, ooo she sings to me, ooo she sings to me.
She says that everything is healing,
that everything is healing.

She says that all of it is love,
that all of it is love,
that all of it is love.

She says don't be afraid of feeling,
don't be afraid of feeling,
that it's okay to feel.

She says that it's all in the balance,
It's all in the balance, It's all in the balance.

She says that everything is worthy,
that everything is worthy,
that everything is worthy,
that everything is worthy,
that everything is worthy.

Las Plantas de Vida de este Medicina se cantan
Ooo se cantan
Las Plantas de Vida de este Medicina se cantan
Ooo se cantan, Ooo se cantan,
Ooo se cantan, Ooo se cantan.

Many thanks to these contributors:

Jarod K. Anderson

A'Marie B. Thomas-Brown

Gloria Cooper

Jason Estes

Benjamin Prasad

Cyrena Giordano/CYRENITY

Susan Grace

Jennifer H.

Darrel Johannes

Topher Kerby

Cody Ray Richardson

Mercy Talley

Marie

Terry Tempest Williams

Le'Vell Zimmerman

Rumi

and the unknown poet

Author page--

Cheryl Lunar Wind lives in the Mount Shasta area in a little town called Weed. She is a practicer of Mayan cosmology, Lakota ceremony, Star Knowledge and the Universal Laws including the Law of One. Her hobbies are writing poetry, music, dance, drum circles and love for all life; plant, animal and crystal. Cheryl has been a guide and spiritual teacher for many years. Now she shares wit and wisdom through poetry, and has published poetry books; Know Your Way, We Are One, Follow the White Rabbit, Love Your Light, LIFE: Shared thru Poetry, Come to Mount Shasta: Sacred Path Poetry, We Are Light, Finding Our Way Home, We Are Forever, Handshake With the Divine, Grand Rising: A New Day Has Dawned, Star Messages: Codes to Sing, Dance and Live by, and now Return to Innocence: Reminders From Spirit.

Testimonials---

"Cheryl's poetry is very inspiring--particularly the way she compares life with the forces of nature. There is a special element in her poems that opens my heart and fills my soul with divine possiblities."
Giovanna Taormina, Co-Founder, One Circle Foundation

"Cheryl's poems have helped me to uncover and honor my own hidden memories. The beauty of her spirit is evident in each tender, insightful passage."
Marguerite Lorimer, www.earthalive.com

"A rare collection filled with raw, courageous honesty. Thought provoking words that will stop you in your tracks."
Snow Thorner, ED Open Sky Gallery, Montague, California

"When wisdom, guidance, confirming comfort, ect. arrives to us humans--from beings with the perspective of other realms--it is a divine gift. Especially in the form of what we call poetry, and through a being with no agenda; Cheryl Lunar Wind simply shares what source gives her!"
--Dragon Love (Thomas) Budde

Cheryl,
Greetings and Happy Monday to you my friend. I just wanted to share with you that every time I read 'Come to Mount Shasta', even now that I'm mentioning it I cry, I cannot help it, it is such a Divine message and so impeccable in its timing. I came up here for Spirit, you know I was called by Source and I live on the mountain and I just want to thank you. Your poem found me last summer at the headwaters during the Alien and Angels conference; and then I found your book sitting in the gazebo and I just can't stop, I love it! I love you, thank you.
---Jim

Cheryl,
Just want to thank you for your bringing me into the community at Shasta. What you are doing/did do is absolutely changing my life. You did it, you were instrumental in helping me set my true path. Spirit is moving and the more of us that listen and act the sooner the shift will be completed.
---Darrel

About Cheryl's poetry--
"You are dynamic! I have known no one who does so much so swiftly, and your writing touches my heart because it comes from your heart."
---The Durwood Show

"Your words are my words. I keep your book 'Know Your Way' on my nightstand. I read it at bedtime and morning."
---Karina Arroyo

"Cheryl's words work magic in my heart, stirring the wisdom that is buried so deeply within me---beautiful indeed!"
---Ellie Pfeiffer, founder of Ellie's Espresso & Bakery, Weed, CA

www.ingramcontent.com/pod-product-compliance
Lightning Source LLC
Chambersburg PA
CBHW061258040426
42444CB00010B/2412